PUFFIN BOOKS

Wicked World!

Some other books by Benjamin Zephaniah

FUNKY CHICKENS
TALKING TURKEYS

BENJAMIN ZEPHANIAH

Wicked World!

Illustrated by
Sarah Symonds

PUFFIN BOOKS

To Brian Patten

PUFFIN BOOKS

Published by the Penguin Group
Penguin Books Ltd, 80 Strand, London WC2R 0RL, England
Penguin Putnam Inc., 375 Hudson Street, New York, New York 10014, USA
Penguin Books Australia Ltd, 250 Camberwell Road, Camberwell, Victoria 3124, Australia
Penguin Books Canada Ltd, 10 Alcorn Avenue, Toronto, Ontario, Canada M4V 3B2
Penguin Books India (P) Ltd, 11 Community Centre, Panchsheel Park, New Delhi – 110 017, India
Penguin Books (NZ) Ltd, Cnr Rosedale and Airborne Roads, Albany, Auckland, New Zealand
Penguin Books (South Africa) (Pty) Ltd, 24 Sturdee Avenue, Rosebank 2196, South Africa

Penguin Books Ltd, Registered Offices: 80 Strand, London WC2R 0RL, England

www.penguin.com

First published 2000

020

Text copyright © Benjamin Zephaniah, 2000
Illustrations copyright © Sarah Symonds, 2000
All rights reserved

The moral right of the author and illustrator has been asserted

Set in Gill Sans Bold

Made and printed in England by Clays Ltd, St Ives plc

British Library Cataloguing in Publication Data
A CIP catalogue record for this book is available from the British Library

ISBN-13: 978-0-14-130683-4

www.greenpenguin.co.uk

CONTENTS

HONGI

They don't mind shaking hands
But you have to understand,
That a really friendly Maori
Wants to Hongi.

It may all seem quite grand
And you may have other plans,
But a really friendly Maori
Wants to Hongi.

After you have exchanged names
It is obviously plain,
That a really friendly Maori
Wants to Hongi.

If you plan to play some games
The house rules are just the same,
You see every friendly Maori
Wants to Hongi.

In New Zealand no one stares
They've been doing it for years,
They know that a really friendly Maori
Wants to Hongi.

Usually it's done in pairs
And it shows how much they care,
So a really friendly Maori
Wants to Hongi.

When the game is lost and won
Even in the midday sun,
Even then a friendly Maori
Wants to Hongi.

It's the way greetings are done
And they can be real good fun,
Yes a really friendly Maori
Wants to Hongi.

If you've just arrived from Belgium
And you have friends in New Zealand,
You should know that friendly Maoris
Want to Hongi.

It don't matter where you come from
It's a most respectful welcome,
You see every friendly Maori
Wants to Hongi.

If you are feeling low
They have ways to make you glow,
Cheer up, every friendly Maori
Wants to Hongi.

They're originals you know
That is why I want to go,
Because every friendly Maori
Wants to Hongi.

BEFORE ALL THESE CITIES

We brave Apache once lived on the plains
Under the hot sun where it hardly rains,
We fought all who came to steal our territory
That is why we are called the brave Apache.

When we did the snake dance we felt like a snake
Not scared of anything and very awake,
We can move as quick as the blink of an eye
We never give up without giving a try.

We wake in the morning and offer a prayer
That says we are thankful for all that is here,
We're thankful for rain, light and big buffalo
We're thankful for movement wherever we go.

Once we were masters of self-education
Now we all live on a dry reservation,
Before all these cities, and factories and trains
We brave Apache once lived on the plains.

THE CELTS

They lived in France and Germany
    The Celts
They lived in France and Germany
    The Celts
They spread their community
Through Holland, Spain and Italy
They left their mark on history
    The Celts.

They moved around for centuries
    The Celts
They moved around for centuries
    The Celts
They moved on land, they moved on sea
From Africa to Brittany
They had great fun in Anglesey
    The Celts.

They worked with silver, bronze and gold
    The Celts
They worked with silver, bronze and gold
    The Celts
The goods they made were bought and sold
Then thrown away when they got old
And they made lucky charms to hold
    The Celts.

They were very agricultural
          The Celts
They were very agricultural
          The Celts
They were functional and pastoral
And really quite exceptional
And they were three-dimensional
          The Celts.

They had a great big empire
          The Celts
They had a great big empire
          The Celts
But just like every empire
For sure it had to expire
They even reigned in Hertfordshire
          The Celts.

They never had an emperor
          The Celts
They never had an emperor
          The Celts
They made homes in Macedonia
Turkey and Transylvania
But they never had an emperor
          The Celts.

They loved their oral poetry
    The Celts
They loved their oral poetry
    The Celts
A great night in for them you see
Was listening to a good story
They really used their memory
    The Celts.

They have languages that still survive
    The Celts
They have languages that still survive
    The Celts
They are a tough and sturdy tribe
In Wales and Scotland they survive
And in Ireland they really thrive
    The Celts.

A MYSTERY FROM HISTORY

Who built that pyramid?
Waz it Joe or waz it Sid?
Waz it Meena or Javid?
Where they old, waz it a kid?

Who built that pyramid?
Waz it Rachel or David?
Waz it built slow or rapid?
Where they well dressed or naked?

Who built that pyramid?
Waz it Johnny or Alfred?
Waz it Assad or Syed?
It's amazing wot they did.

Who built that pyramid?
It's great that they succeeded
Where they single or married?
And who did they build it wid?

VERY MONGOLIAN

The people of Mongolia
Are very, very few,
I went to North Mongolia
And I met one or two,
When I went to the southern parts
I met three, four, or five,
I travelled west on a big brown horse
With built-in overdrive.

When chilly winds went up my nose
I couldn't help but sneeze,
And I couldn't help but notice
That there wasn't any trees,
The mountain and the hillsides there
Were lovely to behold
But I couldn't help but notice
That it was very, very cold.

The people of Mongolia
Are very, very strong,
You have to be when it's that cold
If you want to last for long,
Still, once a year things change
They do have summers there you know,
But you must be quick to see them,
Easy come and easy go.

In Mongolia they have circular homes
That are made of dark timber,
This type of house is moveable
It's what's known as a ger,
And at the centre of the ger
A hole will let in light,
But when I tried to build one
I just couldn't get it right.

Most people in Mongolia
Will own a big warm coat,
And many wise Mongolians
Are humans, sheep and goats,
Mongolia's the kind of place
Where everyone is cool,
And the things that animals leave behind
Are used each day as fuel.

The people of Mongolia
Are very, very few,
I went to East Mongolia
And met another two,
To tell the truth I met much more
Than five or six or seven,
Mongolia's a very, very, very
Cold heaven.

WHOSLAND

At dawn one morn
After eight weeks of sailing,
The Europeans landed
On the gold, sandy beach.

After praying
They made their way
Inland,
With their flags in their hands
And an empire on their minds.

Soon they came across a small village,
All the people came out to see them,
The villagers thought they had come with great
knowledge
And wisdom from afar.
Having never seen Europeans before
This was new and exciting.

When the captain of the ship
Met the elder of the village
He still had a flag in his hand
And an empire on his mind.

'What did you call this land before
we arrived?'
said the captain.

   'Ours'
   said the village elder,

   'Ours.'

HIM IN THE HIMALAYAS

He's quiet
He's careful
He's not a millionaire
He never ever swears,
      Him in the Himalayas.

He smiles
When
He means it
And not because you're there,
He loves you and he cares,
      Him in the Himalayas.

His home is
So simple,
He's happy living there
He's happy he declares,
      Him in the Himalayas.

He's quite close
To nature,
They say he talks to bears
And respects what is theirs,
      Him in the Himalayas.

His robe
Is bright orange
And he don't need no hair,
He doesn't have
    nightmares,
        Him in the Himalayas.

He loves rain
He loves sun
Snow causes no despair,
He does his own repairs,
        Him in the Himalayas.

Have no doubt
He's way out
He lives where most won't
    dare
With very little fears,
        Him in the Himalayas.

He breathes deep
The freshest air,
He's very much aware,
He's always saying prayers,
        Him in the Himalayas.

IN INDONESIA

In Indonesia
There are Moslems and Hindus
In Indonesia
There are Buddhists and Sikhs
In Indonesia
There's more than three hundred tribal groups
Using just as many different ways to speak.

In Indonesia
There's a tribe that's called the Javanese
And another one that's called the Sundanese,
People famous for their batiks are called Balinese
Not to be confused with others known as Madurese.

There are Makasarese, Ambonese and Chinese
There are Torajas and Dayaks and Papuans
And they all live on all these little islands
Eating long grain rice and voicing their opinions.

In Indonesia
Wayang Topeng is masked dance,
And the people are proud of the masks they make,
If you want to go somewhere that's really boring
And you go there
Then you're making a mistake.

In Indonesia
There's shadow plays called Wayang Kulit
And a puppet play is called a Wanyang Golek,
So if you want to find some Indonesian culture
You'll have to learn some new words or
Simply forget it.

FEARLESS BUSHMEN

The bushmen of the Kalahari desert
Painted themselves on rocks
With wildebeests and giraffes
Thousands of years ago.
And still today they say
To boast is sinful
Arrogance is evil.
And although some say today that they
Are the earliest hunter-gatherers known
They never hunt for sport
They think that's rude,
They hunt for food.

They earn respect by sharing
Being true to their word
And caring.
They refuse to own land but
They can build a house in two days
And take it down in four hours.

Three generations will live together.
A girl will grow up to feed her mother
Who feeds the mother
That once fed her.
To get that food a girl will walk
Upon the hot desert sands
An average of a thousand miles a year.

Their footprints are uniquely small
For people who travel so much
To find melons or mongongo trees,
And those small dark and nimble feet
May spend two days chasing a deer.
Charity, respect and tolerance
Are watchwords for these ancient folk
Who spend their evenings singing songs
Around their campfires.

These hunter-gatherers are fearless
But peaceful,
They will never argue with a mamba snake,
When one is seen heading towards the village
They kiss the Earth
And move the village.

GLORIOUS LOSERS

They were mighty warriors
They feared no living thing,
They broke down all barriers
When they were conquering,
Nearly all their enemies
Had to up and run,
When those guys got military
It seems they always won.

When they found a city
They took all that they saw,
They did not have no pity
When they were out at war,
When they met new neighbours
Over the garden wall,
They cut them up with razors
Then enslaved or killed them all.

They battled on the playing fields
They battled in the valley,
They battled with their spears and shields
And even in the alleys,
They would not leave the battleground
Without feeling glorious,
So when some foreign tribes were found
They had to be victorious.

But every now and then it's said
The tables must be turned
And someone may just lose their head
If lessons are not learnt,
These fighters would not tell their foe
They always needed light,
You see the Aztecs of Old Mexico
Just would not fight at night.

When they woke up in the morning
They fought to get some food,
If things were getting boring
They would fight to change the mood,
The men fought over women
And the women fought for men,
When they saw people swimming
They dived in and fought with them.

Throughout Central America
The Aztecs caused such fear,
If you were unfamiliar
They'd make you disappear,
For reasons that we still don't know
(They weren't being polite),
You see the Aztecs of Old Mexico
Just would not fight at night.

The Spanish came one day
And then the Spanish got a beating,
The survivors ran away
But then they came back one fine evening,
The Spanish sent some expert spies
To go and have an expert peep,
Reporting back the spies said, 'Guys,
The Aztecs are all fast asleep!'

To catch the Aztecs off their mark
The Spanish gave no warning,
They got the Aztecs in the dark
When most Aztecs were snoring,
The Aztecs may have been macho
But were they really bright?
You see the Aztecs of Old Mexico
Just would not fight at night.

WAITING FOR ADU

I lost my friend called Adu
I haven't seen him for some time
And I was really worried
He was a great friend of mine.

Adu my friend has gone and
I really miss that kid,
I really miss the funny things
That my mate Adu did.

The last time that I saw him
He was cracking wicked jokes,
We were exchanging stories
Underneath a giant oak.

When I was last with Adu
We were having a great time
Eating nuts and berries
And rapping wicked rhymes.

One day I went to visit him but
His village was not there
And I couldn't see his family
Or his neighbours anywhere.

I shouted out loud, 'Adu,
Hey Adu, where are you?'
The reply was stony silence
And my heart was feeling blue.

I turned to face my village
Then I ran quickly home,
I asked my Mommy why she thought
He left me all alone.

She said, 'Dear son, don't worry and
There's no need to feel sad
That is just his way of life
Adu is a nomad.'

I said, 'What's a nomad, Mommy?'
As I screwed up my face,
She explained to me that nomads
Move around from place to place.

That night when I stopped crying
And I realized it was true,
My Mommy sat and told me of
The things that nomads do.

Some nomads move for food
Some move for the weather
Some move in small family groups
Some large groups move together.

They do not value property
The family must have honour
Most of them do not use money
They just value each other.

Most countries have some nomads
Some people put them down
But since the beginning of time
They have always moved around.

Now I'm not crying for Adu
His going made me learn
Because he is a nomad
One day Adu may return.

THINK CHINESE

Did you know that
  China has more people
  Than anywhere?

China has more mouths to feed
China has more homes,
China has more books to read,
More heads, more hair, more combs,
China has more people
Than anywhere I've known,
So the Chinese have to make sure
That lots of food is grown.
  China has more people
  Than anywhere,
And in China it's hard to be alone.

  China has more people
  Than anywhere.

In China there's more trousers
In China there's more boys,
In China there's more girls
And in China there's more toys,
In China there's more kisses,
Or that's what I've been told,
I really think that this is
A country to behold.
China has more people
Than anywhere,
And most of the people live
To be quite old.

China has more people
Than anywhere.

You should not forget
That China has some wicked verse,
The Chinese alphabet
Is the biggest in the universe,
If all the people in China clapped
The Earth would really shake,
And if all the people in China rapped
Sweet music they would make.
China has more people
Than anywhere,
And that's just one reason why China is great.

VARIETY IS THE SPICE

I've seen some dressed in lightning white
I've seen some dressed in orange robes,
I've seen some dressed dark as the night
In hats and European clothes,
My friend wears shalwar and chemises
With more colours than rainbows on
And I have seen many Jain priests
Who dress to not hurt anyone.

        Millions travel upon their bikes
        And millions travel in their cars
        And millions dream of being like
        Those super Bollywood film stars,
        They dance Hindi, Hip-hop and Jazz
        So people don't believe the hype,
        Because there is no such thing as
        An average Indian stereotype.

They are so rich, they are so poor
And millions are so in-between
Some want for nothing, some want more
And some are quick and very keen,
Some of them wear their hair so short
Some of the girls wear flowered frocks,
In this nation of many sorts
You'll find Sadhus with long dreadlocks.

Some of them live in villages
Some of them live in high-rise flats,
Some of them have big businesses
Some just do bits of this and that,
Sometimes I know that I've been wrong
But now I know that I am right,
Because I know that there's no one
Average Indian stereotype.

Many are wise, many are smart
Many just simply want to be,
Many are light, many are dark
And many of them are just like me,
Many live on cold mountain tops
Many live in the heat below,
Many have no spare time to stop
Many have no spare time to go.

Some of them pray, some of them don't
Some of them sing, some of them won't,
Some of them serve, some of them cook
Some like to read rhymes in a book,
I may not be smart, wise and great
But this time I know I am right,
Make sure that you make no mistake
There is no Indian stereotype.

THE POLE WITH NO SOUL

I'm wondering
How does he do it?
I'm wondering
What is his role?
I'm speaking of my friend Nobody
Nobody lives by the South Pole.

He ain't got no good friends
To talk to
He ain't got nobody to kiss,
There isn't much there
That he can do,
He can't go on living
Like this.

He ain't got no brothers
Or sisters
He ain't got no one
At his side
There's no Mrs
And there's no Mr's
He has no language,
He's from no tribe.

It's so strange to be
With no history
It's so strange that
Nobody's there
I wonder
What his future will be
But Nobody don't seem to care.

Nobody's dancing
He's not on the phone,
There is no music
And he's all alone,
Nobody's eating
Nobody's sharing
Nobody's reading
And Nobody's hearing,
Nobody's not having
The time of his life,
Nobody's talking to
No one from Fife,
Nobody's talking
And saying nothing,
Nobody's a poet
And nobody's singing.

I'm wondering
How does he do it?
It must take
So much self-control,
I'm speaking of my friend Nobody
Nobody lives by the South Pole.

29

THE POLE WITH NO POLES

The North Pole
Is not fit for humans,
You won't find a house
Or a tree,
You won't find Poles,
Germans,
Or Cubans,
The North Pole is right in the sea.

EVERYONE'S FRIEND

My grandad said he was his friend
My grandma said she made him tea,
In Jamaica it seems to me
All grandparents knew Bob Marley.

My cousin said he built his house
My uncle put his carpet down,
My soccer-loving brother Paul
Claims that he kicked Bob Marley's ball.

My teacher said she taught him maths
Some joker said he taught him laughs,
The art school that is understaffed
Still claim they taught him arts and crafts.

My paperboy too has his views,
Said he knows secrets I could use,
When on a Caribbean cruise
He said he brought Bob Marley news.

A playwright in Montego Bay
Said Bob Marley was in her play,
But I could see right from the start
That really he was in her heart.

Rudie said he knew him well
He said he taught him ice hockey,
In Jamaica it seems to me
That all Rudies knew Bob Marley.

The coconut vendors, the pretenders
A smart spider known as Anansi
All the rich who dress up fancy
Now claim that they knew Bob Marley.

Freedom fighters called Maroons
Say that Bob sat in their rooms,
I think the peaceful music maker
Was known by all in Jamaica.

My mother said she made his hats
My auntie cooked his suppers,
An artist with a memory lapse
Said she made him nice bedcovers.

Every copper locked him up
They all said he was nice,
And all the social workers said
They gave Bob some advice.

All the athletes, all the drivers
All the workers, all the skivers,
All the dentists, all the tailors
All the pilots, all the sailors.

Every vet and every baker
Everybody in Jamaica,
Knew the brother personally
Everyone knew Bob Marley.

WE ARE
THE CHEROKEE

We made sacred fires
As instructed
By our ancestors.

We farmed beans
And corn
In harmony
With our surroundings,
We knew the sun well.

We learnt to count
Each drop of rain,
And when we had their number
We thanked the sky
For each drop of rain.

We were so in love
That each one of us
Gave ourselves
And married the Earth.

We are the Cherokee.

Then there came a time
When the land beneath us
Was taken from us.
Even those of us who were not born then
Remember that time.

It was a time of great sadness,
The time of countless tears.

In the state now known as Texas
In the land now known as America
We taught ourselves
To avoid evil thoughts,
And welcome strangers.

Soon after welcoming the strangers
We found we had no land
To welcome strangers.
We learnt the language of the strangers
And tried talk,
Using the language of survival
We tried food,
Then in a desperate bid to save ourselves
We tried self-defence.

Now we live on the land
That we farmed and loved,
On this same piece of land
In a foreign country.

We are the Cherokee.

We can make for you
Beautiful baskets
To carry your dreams.

We can speak to you
In a language
That is older than the country
That contains us.

We can sing you songs
That were taught to us by big buffalo
And running bears,
To music that we gather
From the wind.

The cowboys were not that good
And we were not that bad.
All we wanted was
Our ways
Our names
Ourselves
And peace.

We are the Cherokee.

BENGALI RAP

My friends are very cool
My friends are very wise
Everyone is a winner
Everyone is a prize,
From the city of Dhaka
To the tracts of Chittagong,
My friends are very cool
Like a sweet rap song.

Some live in the city
Some live on the farm
They like to stay cool
They like to stay calm,
They say peace and love to all
Everywhere they go,
If they can say yes
They will never say no.

My friends from Bangladesh
My friends from Bangladesh
They're cool and they're fresh
My friends from Bangladesh.

Sometimes when I have time
I give my friends a call,
And then we all go sailing
In the Bay of Bengal,
That's what you can do
If your friends live by the sea
And if your friends are happy
To play in unity.

Sometimes my good friends
Will come and check me out
And then we get together
To rap, sing and shout,
And then when we get hungry
And we want something nice
We will cook and eat
Some tarka dall and rice.

My friends from Bangladesh
My friends from Bangladesh
They're cool and they're fresh
My friends from Bangladesh.

My friends have got me rocking
Each one is a star
Each one is a lover
And proud of who they are,
I know when they're thinking
That they're thinking of me
And of all the fun we have
With our rap poetry.

And when things get heavy
In the season of monsoons,
We all get together
To shelter in safe rooms,
I hope you get the message
It's loud and it's clear
My good friends are really cool
And they really do care.

My friends from Bangladesh
My friends from Bangladesh
They're cool and they're fresh
My friends from Bangladesh.

THE BRITISH

Serves 60 million

Take some Picts, Celts and Silures
And let them settle,
Then overrun them with Roman conquerors.

Remove the Romans after approximately four
    hundred years
Add lots of Norman French to some
Angles, Saxons, Jutes and Vikings, then stir vigorously.

Mix some hot Chileans, cool Jamaicans, Dominicans,
Trinidadians and Bajans with some Ethiopians,
Chinese, Vietnamese and Sudanese.

Then take a blend of Somalians, Sri Lankans,
    Nigerians
And Pakistanis,
Combine with some Guyanese
And turn up the heat.

Sprinkle some fresh Indians, Malaysians, Bosnians,
Iraqis and Bangladeshis together with some
Afghans, Spanish, Turkish, Kurdish, Japanese
And Palestinians
Then add to the melting pot.

Leave the ingredients to simmer.

As they mix and blend allow their languages to
   flourish
Binding them together with English.

Allow time to be cool.

Add some unity, understanding and respect for the
   future
Serve with justice
And enjoy.

*Note: All the ingredients are equally important. Treating one
ingredient better than another will leave a bitter, unpleasant
taste.*

*Warning: An unequal spread of justice will damage the people
and cause pain.*

      Give justice and equality to all.

A BIG WELCOME

Ladies and gentlemen
Boys and girls,
Put your hands together
And give a
BIG welcome
To the people from the
BIG forest
With the
BIG trees
Welcome
Please
The Pygmies.

Now as you see
The Pygmy is
BIG in Asia
BIG in Africa
And wherever they be
They specialize in living in
BIG harmony
With their neighbours.
So give them a
BIG round of applause,
They hate wars
Say a
BIG hello
To a
BIG hero
Ladies and gentlemen
Boys and girls,
The Pygmies.

KURDISH LAND

A question I keep asking is
Where is Kurdistan?
How come there is a nation
Of people with no land?
I keep asking the question,
It's so hard to understand,
Why some other people
Caused these people to disband.
More than twenty-two million Kurdish folk
Urgently need homes,
They don't want to live off charity,
Hand-outs, beg or live off loans,
It's a shame that all these people,
After all this time,
Have a language that's illegal,
So to speak the truth is a crime.

A question I keep asking is
Where is Kurdistan?
How come this great big nation
Is a nation
Without land?

Roma People Roam

Since leaving northern India
Fifteen hundred years ago
They roamed all over Asia,
Europe and the Americas,
Over Australia and Africa,
The Roma people roam.

People began to call them gypsies,
They thought they came from Egypt
But they did not come from Egypt
Fifteen hundred years ago.
In fact they went all over
From North Africa to Dover
That's so natural for the Roma
The Roma people roam.

At times they have been hated
They have been separated
For not being related
To the people round about,
When things went wrong some blamed them
Without reason they shamed them,
When some folk couldn't tame them
What they did was throw them out.

It's said that some could read your future
Without knowing your past,
And they used to be famous
For all their arts and crafts,
It's said that this nomadic people
Have trod a million paths
Trading as they go
The Roma people roam.

These people have been everywhere
That human beings can go
Since leaving northern India
Fifteen hundred years ago,
So throughout the world you'll hear them
Singing in joyful tones,
And throughout the world you'll see them
Living in their homes,
People throughout the world will see them
Going straight through no-go zones,
Everywhere
The Roma people roam.

URDU POETS

Urdu poets speak wonders,
They are like magical wordsmiths,
They pluck words out of the sky
And create something for you to live for.

Urdu poets have a heavenly language
A language created by poets for poets,
A language that has turned a nation into poets,
Poets that love to speak to each other.

They bring glory to the bazaars
Hope to the pavements
Libraries to the mind,
They light up dark wordless days
Adding joy to eyes that are sad.
Urdu poets have been known to create paradise
In downtown Karachi
And wordplay on cricket fields,
Their verse so full of grace
Even when it is angry Urdu is beautiful.

Combine fire with water
Combine the calm with the storm,
Combine the greatest painters
With the greatest subjects
And you will have Urdu poets.

Knowledge can be tasty
To question can be delightful.

VOICES FOR CHOICES

If you did not have a car
You could still walk,
If you did not have a phone
You could still talk,
If you did not have a batter
Then the cricket would not matter
And you could still eat all your greens
Without a fork.

You could have a great big telly
With no vision,
We could all live without crime
And without prison,
Without dark we'd just have light
Without light we'd just have night
And if we tried we could eat cakes
That have not risen.

If we did not have cartoons
We'd all be funny,
And we'd probably be more equal
Without money,
We could live without computers
Dictators and persecutors
And our lives could still be quite sweet
Without honey.

But I'm trying to make sure
No one forgets,
That we really needed
Mighty Suffragettes,
If they did not raise their voices
Most of us would have no choices
And I think that we'd have many
Deep regrets.

INUIT

We live on top of the world.
From the icy deserts of Alaska
To the icy villages of Siberia
We are one,
We are at home.
Our lands are white and cold
American and European,
We are a close-knit
Far-flung tribe.
But we will not let distance
Or the weather
Hold us back,
If our snowmobiles struggle
And our motorboats freeze
Our dogs will take us quickly,
When electricity is low
And we have no gas to go
Our native dogs will rise up
And ride on.

There comes a time in every year
When many of us see no dusk,
The sun will shine for twenty-four hours one day
And then twenty-four hours the next day
Leaving no time for darkness
No hours for night.
This kind of sun is hot
Enough to warm our hearts
But it will not melt our future,
It lights the way
But it will not blind us,

This kind of sun
Reminds us of our place
On this planet.

Our name means people
Borders mean nothing
And the treatment of the fish we eat
Means everything to we who have no greens.
We can feel the past
We can carry the past with us but
We will not live in a frozen past
Unwilling to look beyond today,
Nor will we die in the fast lane
Of the super-modern highway.

In Greenland and Canada
We have roots,
We have relatives in tomorrow,
That is why as we look back
We look forward,
And as we look skywards
We look down.

Look up dear friends
And wave to us,
We live on top of the world.

THE VEGANS

That man is really trying
To watch what he is buying,
So long as he is able
He will read every label,
He wants to know what's in
Each packet and each tin,
Before he hits the streets
He's checking out the eats.

That woman plants and grows
Then she reaps what she sows,
In order not to panic
She tries to eat organic,
She doesn't think she's perfect
But she thinks she's worth it,
She likes nice food that's memorable
Not bad food that's chemical.

Take a good look at that boy
Does he not fill you with joy?
He's trying to explain
That the thing he hates is pain,
That boy will never wear
Any fox fur or horsehair,
He will not follow fashion
His main thing is compassion.

That girl will not eat haddock
Or any animal product,
She's even learnt to think
About her bedtime drink,
She makes sure that her cuisine
Has the vitamins and protein
To keep her strong and healthy
Even if she is not wealthy.

All these people share
Concern for what they wear,
They check their shopping trolleys
And what goes in their bodies,
They are not all one colour
And it seems they live all over,
You see there are many reasons
Why these people are vegans.

WHO ARE WE?

So who are you?

Are you one of those
Tall people?
Are you one of those
Black people?
Or are you just one of
Those people,
Those other people,
You know
Them people?

We are calling us
Disabled people,
Able-bodied people,
Rich people,
Poor people,
Upper class people
Middle class people
Working class people
And even
Lower class people.

Who do we think we are?

We call some people
Foreign people,
Strange people,
Different people,
Why do we still
Label people?
Why do some people feel like
Chosen people?

OK
I know we come from different places,
We have different shades of skin,
And there are different ways of living
In the countries we live in,
And
Some people can do some things
And some people can do others,
But I think that we have to see
We're all sisters and brothers
And

Children may be small people
Adults may be big people
But when you get right down to it
All people are people,
And
As far as I can see
You're all related to me,
That is why I say that
All people are equal.

Now let your reply be true
Everybody
Who are you?

MY FRIEND MOUNTAIN FLOWER

She dresses in a thousand beads
  Each year she plants a thousand seeds.

With skill she weaves her wicker baskets
  She weaves her people's sleeping blankets.

She may not have what we call wealth
  But she can build her house herself.

Although she still lives with her Mom
  Experts can't work out where she's from.

She comes from a village people,
  They're famous for being peaceful.

If she gets married she won't roam
  Her husband must live in her home.

Some say that with the passing years
  Her way of life just disappears.

She's my friend, and you can quote me,
  Mountain Flower is a Hopi.

WE KNOW

Monkeys are not doing it,
Snakes are not doing it,
Neither are beetles or fleas,
Lizards are not doing it,
Birds are not doing it,
They know that we need the trees,
Mice are not doing it,
Lice are not doing it,
Cats are not doing it
Honest,
Bats are not doing it,
I know who's doing it,
Humans are killing the forest.

THE MAASAI GIRLS

The Maasai girls are dancing
And the earth is moving.

The Maasai girls are dancing
And there's thunder under feet.

The Maasai girls are dancing
And the mountains are alive,
Because the great dance of the tribe has just begun.

The Maasai girls are dancing
In Tanzania.

The Maasai girls dance beautiful
In Kenya.

The Maasai girls are dancing
And the boys are all amazed,
The Maasai girls are dancing in the sun.

A GRIOT WRITES

A Griot,
On the Streets,
In Villages,
Towns and Cities,
Senegal,
West Africa.

Dear People,

I hope that you are all well wherever you may be and
that peace and love is in your lives.

Before coming to my main reason for writing to you, I
would like to make it clear that we griots are not
restricted to any one tribe, country or religion, and
although we originate in the western parts of Africa,
our offspring are taking our traditions to Europe,
Australia and the American continent.

I have reason to believe that many of you around the
world do not quite understand who we griots are and
what we do. I have heard that your people-experts are
a little confused by our role in our society.

A griot can be female or male, young or old. Many of
us have been trained by our parents or the elders in
our neighbourhoods and we will do our work for the
rest of our lives. We are storytellers, it is our job to
keep the ancient stories alive and sometimes we
introduce new stories to deal with new subjects. We
are poets, it is our job to keep the language alive by
using wordplay and words that are beautiful and
rhythmic. We are singers, we can play many

instruments and sing many old and new songs for you. Some of our songs will be on traditional instruments and some of our griots use modern guitars and drums. You can be a griot and even sing Rock 'n' Roll, Soul, Reggae or Jazz, as long as it is done in the right spirit and with respect to the people. Many griots mix these styles with our local African music. We are historians, keeping alive memories from the past; we are prophets, looking forward into the future; we are dancers at weddings and other great ceremonies; we are actors on the stage of reality and we are newscasters. If our rulers are not being completely honest, or in areas where there are no newspapers and television, we are the ones who tell people what is really happening in the world.

So you see, people, we griots are many things, we are not just poets, or singers, dancers, or actors, we are all-round commentators, who work for the good of our community and not just for money. We are the oral tradition.

I really do hope this letter goes some way in helping you to understand exactly what a griot is, and how important our work is to us and our people.

By the way, we griots are comedians too. If I see you in Africa I'll tell you a joke that will make you laugh your chin off. But I don't want to talk about that now.

Say hello to your peace of the earth from me, and don't forget to kiss the sky.

Yours sincerely,

A Griot

IN THE MOUNTAINS OF TIBET

In the mountains of Tibet
It seems they won't forget
Their customs and their karma
And the Dalai Lama.
These non-violent monks and nuns
Fight for peace without big guns,
And non-violence makes them calmer,
As calm as the Dalai Lama.
As the farmer herds his yaks
The farmer knows the facts,
And that is why the farmer
Longs to see the Dalai Lama,
Yes it seems that in Tibet
Children simply won't forget
Their customs and their karma
And the Dalai Lama.

THE TOURISTS ARE COMING

Tell them to be careful
If they're not give them an earful
The tourists are coming
The tourists are coming.

They may want to party nightly
But tell them they must be tidy
The tourists are coming
The tourists are coming.

They must respect what we've planted
They should not take us for granted
The tourists are coming
The tourists are coming.

They should practise what they preach
When they're lying on our beach
The tourists are coming to play.

Because our land is sunny
They come here with their money
The tourists are coming
The tourists are coming.

We will not rant and rave
If they will behave
The tourists are coming
The tourists are coming.

We will not be bitter
If they don't drop their litter
    The tourists are coming
    The tourists are coming.

If they don't mess about
We will not kick them out
The tourists are coming to stay.

If by chance you see some
Try to make them welcome
    The tourists are coming
    The tourists are coming.

If they treat us good
They're welcome in the neighbourhood
    The tourists are coming
    The tourists are coming.

But if they're out of order
Show them to the border
    The tourists are coming
    The tourists are coming.

And if it does start raining
Tell them off if they're complaining
The tourists are coming I say.

Tell them that we love living
And money can't buy everything
The tourists are coming
The tourists are coming.

Call them names like fools and criminals
If they don't respect our animals
The tourists are coming
The tourists are coming.

Tell them if they can't keep the peace
That tourism may have to cease
The tourists are coming
The tourists are coming.

Tell them not to be greedy
And be careful where they wee wee
The tourists are coming this way.

PEOPLE NEED PEOPLE

To walk to
To talk to
To cry and rely on,
People will always need people.
To love and to miss
To hug and to kiss,
It's useful to have other people.
To whom will you moan
If you're all alone,
It's so hard to share
When no one is there,
There's not much to do
When there's no one but you,
People will always need people.

To please
To tease
To put you at ease,
People will always need people.
To make life appealing
And give life some meaning,
It's useful to have other people.
If you need a change
To whom will you turn,
If you need a lesson
From whom will you learn,
If you need to play
You'll know why I say
People will always need people.

As girlfriends
As boyfriends,
From Bombay
To Ostend,
People will always need people.
To have friendly fights with
And share tasty bites with,
It's useful to have other people.
People live in families
Gangs, posses and packs,
It seems we need company
Before we relax,
So stop making enemies
And let's face the facts,
People will always need people,
Yes
People will always need people.

CHILDREN OF THE SEWERS

Nobody knows how many children
Live in stinking sewers,
The experts have lost count of how many
Children, beg, steal and die
In the stinking sewers.
Some people don't even call
Children who live in the sewers children,
They call them vermin and filth,
Tramps and thieves.
Unable to understand what it's like to live
In nooks and crannies,
They step over, walk over, walk around
Bypass and ignore these children,
Who could be their children
Before they know it.
Unwilling to lend a hand
They make themselves busy,
Too busy to lend a hand,
They wrap themselves in big houses
Big cars, big money, big swimming pools,
And they have big fences
To stop them seeing
The small children
Who live in the stinking sewers.

Ask the children of the sewers
Why they live in the sewers
And you will hear horror stories,
Stories of loveless lives,
Stories of rejection,
Stories of abuse,
These children's only fault
Was having the wrong parents.

So if there are children living in the sewers
In your city,
Or if you see the children of the sewers
On television,
Before you walk by or
Change channels,
Just think of how lucky you are,
Think of where your waste is going
Think of what you do with what you don't want,
And remember that sewers
Were not made for children,
But then again nor were violent homes,
Families that don't care
Or people that don't respect children.
You don't need the World Health Organization
To tell you that a sewer is one of
The most unsafe places in a city,
But for some children
A stinking unsafe sewer
Is the safest place they know.

SIGHTS AND SOUNDS

**There are
More than
Six thousand
Different
Languages
Spoken
On Earth.**

**There is
No person
On Earth
Who can speak
Them all.**

**Every person
On Earth
Could learn
To speak
Any language
On Earth.**

**There are
Some languages
That are not
Spoken.**

Languages
Like people
Have family trees.

Languages
Like people
Are all precious.

Languages
Like people
Can disappear.

Languages are
Like people

Respect your tongue.

Sign languages
Are
Crucial

Protect your hands.

ONE FOUR ALL

There are
More than
Six billion
Individual
People
On Earth.

There is
No one person
Who knows
Every person
On Earth.

Every person
On Earth
Could spend
Their whole life
Learning
About themselves.

Some people
Spend their lives
Teaching people
To be people.

People
Like languages
Have family trees.

People
All over
Are all gorgeous.

People
Like languages
Can disappear.

People are
Like you

Respect people.

All people
Are
Vital

Protect people.

EVERY BODY IS DOING IT

In Hawaii they Hula
They Tango in Argentina
They Reggae in Jamaica
And they Rumba down in Cuba,
In Trinidad and Tobago
They do the Calypso
And in Spain the Spanish
They really do Flamenco.

In the Punjab they Bhangra
How they dance Kathak in India
Over in Guatemala
They dance the sweet Marimba,
Even foxes dance a lot
They invented the Fox Trot,
In Australia it's true
They dance to the Didgeridoo.

In Kenya they Benga
They Highlife in Ghana
They dance Ballet all over
And Rai dance in Algeria,
They Jali in Mali
In Brazil they Samba
And the girls do Belly Dancing
In the northern parts of Africa.

Everybody does the Disco
From Baghdad to San Francisco
Many folk with razzamataz
Cannot help dancing to Jazz,
They do the Jig in Ireland
And it is really true
They still Morris dance in England
When they can find time to.

WE REFUGEES

I come from a musical place
Where they shoot me for my song
And my brother has been tortured
By my brother in my land.

I come from a beautiful place
Where they hate my shade of skin
They don't like the way I pray
And they ban free poetry.

I come from a beautiful place
Where girls cannot go to school
There you are told what to believe
And even young boys must grow beards.

I come from a great old forest
I think it is now a field
And the people I once knew
Are not there now.

We can all be refugees
Nobody is safe,
All it takes is a mad leader
Or no rain to bring forth food,
We can all be refugees
We can all be told to go,
We can be hated by someone
For being someone.

I come from a beautiful place
Where the valley floods each year
And each year the hurricane tells us
That we must keep moving on.

I come from an ancient place
All my family were born there
And I would like to go there
But I really want to live.

I come from a sunny, sandy place
Where tourists go to darken skin
And dealers like to sell guns there
I just can't tell you what's the price.

I am told I have no country now
I am told I am a lie
I am told that modern history books
May forget my name.

We can all be refugees
Sometimes it only takes a day,
Sometimes it only takes a handshake
Or a paper that is signed.
We all came from refugees
Nobody simply just appeared,
Nobody's here without a struggle,
And why should we live in fear
Of the weather or the troubles?
We all came here from somewhere.

I LUV ME MUDDER

I luv me mudder an me mudder luvs me
   We cum so far from over de sea,
We heard dat de streets were paved wid gold
   Sometimes it's hot, sometimes it's cold,
I luv me mudder an me mudder luvs me
   We try fe live in harmony
Yu might know her as Valerie
   But to me she's just my mummy.

She shouts at me daddy so loud sometime
   She's always been a friend of mine
She's always doing de best she can
   She works so hard down ina Englan,
She's always singin sum kinda song
   She has big muscles an she very, very strong,
She likes pussycats an she luvs cashew nuts
   An she don't bother wid no if an buts.

I luv me mudder an me mudder luvs me
   We come so far from over de sea,
We heard dat de streets were paved wid gold
   Sometimes it's hot, sometimes it's cold,
I luv her and whatever we do
   Dis is a luv I know is true,
My people, I'm talking to yu
   Me an my mudder we luv yu too.

BRIGHT AND BEAUTIFUL

Sun shines
> Stars shine

Moon shines.

Trees shine
> Life shines

Good shines.

Day shines
> Night shines

Earth shines

White shines
> Black shines

You shine.

Confessions of a Runner

On my first day at school
  My sister cried and cried
On my first day at school
  I could have died and died
On my first day at school
  My twin embarrassed me
On my first day at school
  I learnt schoolology.

On my second day at school
  My sister wouldn't come
On my second day at school
  She was dragged there by my Mom
On my second day at school
  I came dressed in pink
On my second day at school
  I was made to think.

On my third day at school
  I explored everywhere
On my third day at school
  I fell offa my chair
On my third day at school
  We all went for a swim
On my third day at school
  I cried just like my twin.

On my fourth day at school
  They made me run in shorts
On my fourth day at school
  I discovered sports
On my fourth day at school
  I ran fast and far
On my fourth day at school
  I earned myself a star.

On my fifth day at school
  We had tomato crumble
On my fifth day at school
  I began to grumble
On my fifth day at school
  My teacher got stuck in red tape
On my fifth day at school
  Me and my twin escaped.

THERE'S SOMEONE

It may not be the one you're with
They may not have much love to give,
It may not be the girl next door
Or that nice boy on the first floor,
It may not be the friend you taught
Who helps you out when you're distraught,
You may not know this one that well
But there's someone who loves you.

It may not be the one you kissed
It may not be the one you've missed,
You may think someone is your friend
But then you find that they pretend,
When you are down and you are out
When you're in tears, sad, and in doubt,
Life may feel like a living hell
But there's someone who loves you.

JAMAICAN SUMMERS

Jamaican summers are so hot,
But all over Jamaica
People walk around saying
Dis is cool
Dat is cool
She is cool
Or he's so cool.

Jamaican summers are so hot,
Dat all over Jamaica
Parents are always saying
Drink yu coconut water
Drink yu kisko pops
Drink yu mountain water
Yu muss drink a lot.

Jamaican summers are so hot,
Dat all over Jamaica
People chill out in de shade
Sleep under trees
Or travel fe miles
To find cool breeze.

In Jamaica,
Very soon after summer
Comes de winter,
But beware
Let me give yu a warning me friend,
Jamaican winters are so hot.

WE PEOPLE TOO

I have dreams of summer days
Of running freely on the lawn
I luv a lazy Sunday morn
Like many others do.
I luv my family always
I luv clear water in a stream
Oh yes I cry and yes I dream
We dogs are people too.

When I have time I luv sightseeing
You may not want to see my face
But you and me must share a space
Like many others do.
Please think of me, dear human being,
It seems that I'm always in need
I have a family to feed
We mice are people too.

They say we're really dangerous
But we too like to feel and touch
And we like music very much
Like many others do.
Most of us are not poisonous
I have a little lovely face
I move around with style and grace
We snakes are people too.

And I, dear folk, am small and great
My friends call me the mighty Bruce
I luv to drink pure orange juice
Like many others do.
I hope you all appreciate
We give you all a helping hand
When me and my friends turn the land
We worms are people too.

I don't mind if you stand and stare
But know that I have luv no end
And my young ones I will defend
Like many others do.
When you see me in the air
Remember that I know the worth
Of all us who share the earth
We birds are people too.

I need fresh air and exercise
I need to safely cross the road,
I carry such a heavy load
Like many others do.
Don't only judge me by my size
Ask any veterinarian
I'm just a vegetarian
We cows are people too.

Water runs straight off my smooth back
And I hold my head high with pride
I like my children at my side
Like many others do.
I don't care if you're white or black
If you like land or air or sea
I want to see more unity
We ducks are people too.

I think living is so cool
And what I really like the most
Is kiss chase and I luv brown toast
Like many others do.
I hang around in a big school
I only need a little sleep
I like thinking really deep
We fish are people too.

I luv the cows I love the trees
And I would rather you not smoke
For if you smoke then I would choke
Like many others do.
I beg you do not squash me please
I do not want to cause you harm
I simply want you to stay calm
We flies are people too.

My name is Thomas Tippy Tops
Billy is not my name
I've learnt to live with fame
Like many others do.
I once was on Top of the Pops
On TV I sang loud
My parents were so proud
We goats are people too.

I luv to walk among the fern
I'm thankful for each night and day
I really luv to holiday
Like many others do.
I've read the books and my concern
Is why do we always look bad?
My friends don't think I'm raving mad
We wolves are people too.

A lovely garden makes me smile
A good joke makes me croak
One day I want to own a boat
Like many others do.
I'd luv to see the river Nile
I'd luv my own sandcastle
I really want to travel
We frogs are people too.

Please do not call me horrid names
Think of me as a brother
I'm quite nice you'll discover
Like many others do.
If you're my friend then call me James
I'll be your friend for ever more
I'll be the one that you adore
We pigs are people too.

We really need this planet
And we want you to be aware
We just don't have one spare
Not any of us do.

We dogs, we goats
We mice, we snakes
Even we worms
Are really great,
We birds, we cows
We ducks, we frogs
Are just trying to do our jobs
We wolves, we fish
We pigs, we flies
Could really open up your eyes
And all we want to say to you
Is that
We all are people too.

Be Cool Mankind

My love for you
 Is oh so true,
Be good mankind, be good mankind,
And let us be as one people,
 Be good mankind, be good.

Let's live some more
 Abandon war,
 Be safe mankind, be safe mankind,
 And let us live our dreams people,
 Be safe mankind, be safe.

There is one race
 The living race,
Spread love mankind, spread love mankind,
And let's be peace and love people
 Spread love mankind, spread love.

Don't get me wrong
 My love is strong,
Be cool mankind, be cool mankind,
And let us live as one people,
 Be cool mankind, be cool.

Index of First Lines